Note to Parents and Teachers

The READING ABOUT: STARTERS series introduces key science vocabulary and concepts to young children while encouraging them to discover and understand the world around them. The series works as a set of graded readers in three levels.

LEVEL 3: READ ALONE follows guidelines set out in the National Curriculum for Year 3 in schools. These books can be read alone or as part of guided or group reading. Each book has three sections:

• Information pages that introduce key concepts. Key words appear in bold for easy recognition on pages where the related science concepts are explained.
• A lively story that recalls this vocabulary and encourages children to use these words when they talk and write.
• A quiz asks children to look back and recall what they have read.

ANTS to WHALES looks at THE ANIMAL KINGDOM. Below are some answers and activities related to the questions on the information spreads that parents, carers and teachers can use to discuss and develop further ideas and concepts:

p. 4 *Collect pictures of animals. Sort them into these six main groups.* You could introduce other groups such as crustaceans and molluscs.

p. 6 *Why do you think backbones are not just one long bone?* Get children to explore different parts of their skeleton, e.g. to look for biggest/smallest bone. You could expand this by talking about how muscles and bones work together to help animals move.

p. 9 *Can you think of animals that swim, slither, creep, crawl or scuttle?* Encourage children to explore and expand their vocabulary. You could play a game where they try to match words for movement with particular animals or enact the movements.

p. 11 *What flying insects visit flowers?* You could mention how animals and plants live and work together. Plants produce sweet nectar/fruits/nuts so that animals will help them to pollinate/scatter their seeds.

p. 13 *What other than a car or shark has a long, smooth shape?* Ask children to link animals and machines e.g. bird and plane, fish and submarine. You could also mention the smooth body suits that some athletes wear to help them swim or run faster.

p. 17 *What happens to your old skin?* It flakes off. You could also expand by comparing with changes in other animals as they grow, e.g. frog, butterfly, grasshopper.

p. 19 *Does it (a feather) feel light or heavy?* You could also mention that feathers keep birds warm and dry and that feathers need care, e.g. birds oil and wash their feathers.

ADVISORY TEAM

Educational Consultant
Andrea Bright – Science Co-ordinator, Trafalgar Junior School, Twickenham

Literacy Consultant
Jackie Holderness – former Senior Lecturer in Primary Education, Westminster Institute, Oxford Brookes University

Series Consultants
Anne Fussell – Early Years Teacher and University Tutor, Westminster Institute, Oxford Brookes University

David Fussell – C.Chem., FRSC

CONTENTS

4   Animal Kingdom

6   Backbones and Vertebrates

8   Invertebrates

10   Insects

12   Fish

14   Amphibians

16   Reptiles

18   Birds

20   Mammals

22   Learning

24   **Story: Nature Safari**
What animals can Owen and
Sara track down near their home?

31   Quiz

32   Index

© Aladdin Books Ltd 2005

Designed and produced by
Aladdin Books Ltd
2/3 Fitzroy Mews
London W1T 6DF

First published in
Great Britain in 2005 by
Franklin Watts
96 Leonard Street
London EC2A 4XD

A catalogue record for this
book is available from the
British Library.

ISBN 0 7496 6249 2 (H'bk)

ISBN 0 7496 6382 0 (P'bk)

Editor: Jim Pipe
Design: Flick, Book Design
and Graphics

Thanks to:
• The pupils of Trafalgar Infants
School, Twickenham, for
appearing as models in this book.
• Lynne Thompson for helping to
organise the photoshoots.
• The pupils and teachers of
Trafalgar Junior School,
Twickenham and St. Nicholas
C.E. Infant School, Wallingford,
for testing the sample books.

Photocredits:
l-left, r-right, b-bottom, t-top,
c-centre, m-middle
Cover tl & tr, 2bl, 7tr, 18b, 19tr,
23mr, 27t, 31bl — Stockbyte. Cover
tm, 15b, 16tr — Photodisc. Cover
main, 2ml, 5tc, 9m, 12t, 13t, 13m,
18tr, 20tr, 20b, 22b — Corbis. 2tl,
3, 8b, 10b, 14b, 16mr, 29ml, 29br,
31ml, 31ml — Digital Vision. 4,
31tr — Comstock. 5tl, 5tr, 5bl, 5br,
9b, 15m, 17tl, 21mr, 24mr, 25b,
26br — Ingram Publishing. 5bc,
7br, 12b, 21t, 23br, 30mr, 31bc,
31bl — John Foxx Images. 6t, 17b,
25t — Select Pictures. 6b — PBD.
7m, 16b, 17br, 30tl — Flick Smith.
8t, 10t, 10b — Otto Rogge
Photography. 9t, 21bl — NOAA.
10-11, 26ml — USDA. 13b — US
Navy. 14t, 19b, 24b, 26tr, 27b —
Jim Pipe. 15t, 23tr — Corel. 19tl,
28t, 29tr — US Fish & Wildlife
Service. 22tr — Brand X Pictures.
28br — David Jones.

ANIMAL KINGDOM

Ants to Whales

by Sally Hewitt

Aladdin/Watts
London • Sydney

ANIMAL KINGDOM

Animals can be found everywhere on Earth, from the tops of mountains to deep under the sea.

Human

There are about two million different kinds of animal. They all belong to the **animal kingdom**.

You are a kind of animal called a human.

Dog

Collect pictures of animals. Then sort them into the groups on page 5.

What group do humans and dogs belong to?

Scientists have sorted the **animal kingdom** into groups. Here are some of the biggest groups.

Fish
Sharks, goldfish and salmon are fish.

Insects
Beetles, butterflies, ants and bees are insects.

Amphibians
Toads, frogs and newts are amphibians.

Birds
Ducks, eagles and seagulls are birds.

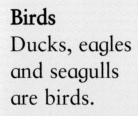

Reptiles
Lizards, snakes and turtles are reptiles.

Mammals
Rabbits, seals and elephants are mammals.

BACKBONES AND VERTEBRATES

You have a row of knobbly bones down the middle of your back. This is your **backbone**. It is also called a spine.

This is part of your skeleton. Your skeleton gives you a shape and keeps you upright.

Animals with a **backbone** are called **vertebrates**.

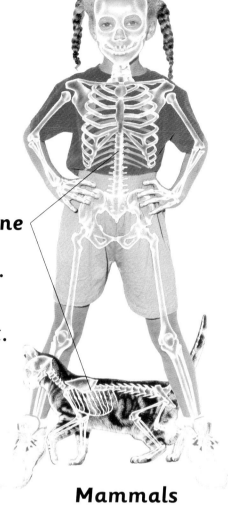

Backbone

Mammals

Imagine what your body would be like without bones.

Feel your backbone while you move your back. Why do you think that backbones are not just one long bone?

Mammals, reptiles, birds and fish are all **vertebrates**. They all have a **backbone**.

Reptile   **Bird**

A **backbone** is made up of lots of small bones. A crocodile is very long. Its **backbone** goes from its tail up to its head.

Fish

INVERTEBRATES

Some animals do not have a backbone.
They are called **invertebrates**.
They have soft bodies with no skeleton
inside them.

A scorpion has a skeleton on
the outside of its soft body.

A snail has a hard shell
to protect it.

Snail   **Scorpion**

Many strange-shaped **invertebrates** live underwater, such as squid and jellyfish.

They don't have legs, fins or flippers. They move around in all kinds of unusual ways.

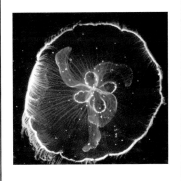

Can you see any bones inside this jellyfish?

Squid

A starfish walks across the rocks using the tiny suckers on its feet.

What animals move in these ways: swim, slither, creep, crawl, scuttle?

Starfish

9

INSECTS

Insects are invertebrates.
They have a body with three parts:
the head, thorax and abdomen.

Insects have a hard case
outside their bodies.
This case protects them
like a suit of armour.

Insects always have six
legs and most have wings.

Beetle

Head

Thorax

Abdomen

Why isn't a spider
an insect? Count its
legs and find out!

All **insects** lay eggs. The eggs hatch into young called larvae. As they grow, the larvae change into the adult **insect**.

Larvae

What flying insects visit flowers?

Take a look at flying insects, but be careful not to disturb them. Bees and wasps can sting!

FISH

Fish live underwater all their lives. They breathe oxygen in the water, using gills on each side of their head.

Fish lay eggs which hatch into little fish.

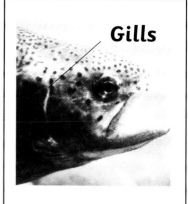

Gills

You can see a fish's gills moving on the side of its head.

Fin

Tail

Eye

Gills

Many **fish** have a long, smooth body. This is a good shape for swimming fast through water.

Fish have strong tails to push them along. Their fins to help them steer.

This fish has a flat shape so it can hide in the sand.

Shark

What is similar about the shape of a racing car and a shark?

What else can you think of that has a long, smooth shape?

13

AMPHIBIANS

Amphibians are animals that have lives in two parts. A frog is an **amphibian.** It spends the first part of its life as a tadpole swimming underwater.

It spends the second part of its life as a frog. It swims in water and hops on land.

Frog

Tadpoles have gills and a tail like a fish.

Newt

Toad

Toads and newts are also **amphibians**.

Adult **amphibians** breathe air, so when they are underwater they must come up to breathe.

They lay their eggs in water so they do not dry out.

If you had very long legs like a frog, how would you move on land?

Can you kick your legs like a frog when you are swimming?

REPTILES

Reptiles have dry, scaly, waterproof skins. They use energy from the Sun to keep warm.

Lizards and crocodiles bask in the Sun to warm up. Some float in the water to cool down.

Lizard

You keep warm from the energy in your food.

Tortoises and turtles
are **reptiles** with a shell.
They move very slowly!

Tortoise

Snake

Snakes are **reptiles**
with no legs.

Most snakes move
from side to side to
slither along the
ground.

Reptiles lay their eggs on the ground.
Young reptiles look just like adult reptiles.

**Old snake
skin**

As they grow, snakes keep shedding their
old skin. What happens to your old skin?

Snake eggs

BIRDS

Birds are the only animals that have feathers. Instead of arms, they have wings.

Birds flap their wings to fly and spread them out to soar through the air.

Not all birds fly. A penguin uses its wings like flippers. They help it to swim.

Duck eggs   **Blackbird chicks**

Birds lay eggs and sit on them to keep them warm. Inside the eggs, the growing chicks feed on the white and the yolk.

When the chicks hatch, the mother and father **bird** feed them until they can fly away.

Feathers push the air when a bird flaps its wings.

Hold a feather in your hand. Does it feel light or heavy? Why is this important?

Feather

MAMMALS

Most **mammals** have hair on their bodies. They sweat to keep cool. All **mammals** breathe air.

Mammals can look very different. Bats are **mammals** with wings. Whales and seals have flippers.

Bat

Some mammals have thick hair on their bodies called fur.

Fur helps to keep this seal warm even in cold, icy places.

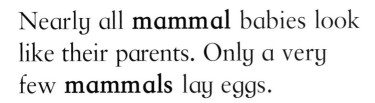

Gibbon

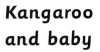
Kangaroo and baby

Nearly all **mammal** babies look like their parents. Only a very few **mammals** lay eggs.

All baby **mammals** drink milk from their mothers. Some grow up in a pouch, like a baby kangaroo.

Enormous blue whales are the largest mammals.

They spend their lives in the sea but swim to the surface to breathe air.

Do you know what the biggest animal on land is?

21

LEARNING

A baby elephant **learns** from its mother. It stays with her until it is old enough to look after itself.

Humans **learn** as we grow. We are the only animals that use words to talk and write.

You can learn from books as well as from your parents.

Elephant

What do you see, hear and smell with? This cow gives you some big clues.

Which parts of your body do you taste or feel with?

Animals use their senses to **learn** what is going on around them.

Many animals smell, taste and feel in different ways from you.

Insects use their antennae. Cats use their whiskers. Snakes use their tongues.

Insect's antennae

Snake's tongue

Cat's whiskers

23

NATURE SAFARI

Look out for animals from different groups in the animal kingdom.

"I wish we could go on safari and see lions or tigers!" said Sara. She shut her book and sighed.

"I'll take you on safari," said Mum. "Will we see lions or tigers?" asked Owen. "No, but we'll see all kinds of amazing animals," said Mum.

They each packed a rucksack. Owen took a magnifying glass, camera and binoculars.

Sara packed a notebook and coloured pencils. "I'll take water, apples and sandwiches," said Mum.

"One point for every animal we spot," said Sara.
"One point to me then," said Mum, looking at Sara and Owen.

"We're not animals," said Owen.
"Yes, you are," said Mum.
"Humans are animals."

They walked through the forest. "I can't see any animals!" said Owen. "Be patient," said Mum. "Stand very still. Look all around you and listen."

"Most animals are shy," said Sara.

"Even a big deer will run away if it hears, sees or smells us."

"What are these?" asked Owen.
"Rabbit droppings," said Mum.
"Shush!" said Sara.
"Look in that field."

Owen looked through the binoculars.
"Hundreds of rabbits!" he said. Suddenly, the
rabbits all ran away.

"It's a fox," said Mum.
"He's frightened them away."
Sara wrote rabbits and fox
in her notebook.

"One point to me for
the rabbits. And one
point to Mum for the
fox," she said.

"And a point to me for
spotting the droppings!"
laughed Owen.

26

"Listen!" said Mum.

They heard a rustling sound above them.

"What's that?" said Sara.

Owen looked through the binoculars. "It's a thrush," he said. "I can see its speckled breast."

"Let me see," said Sara taking the binoculars. "It's feeding a worm to its chicks!" she said.

"I saw the thrush. One point to me!" shouted Owen.

The thrush flew away.

"Shush! Remember to be quiet!" said Sara.

27

"We've seen mammals and birds so far,"
said Sara looking at her notebook.

"That pond looks like a good place to spot all
kinds of animals," said Mum. "But be careful.
Don't go too near the edge."

"What's in the water?
It looks like spotty
jelly!" said Sara.
"It's frogspawn,"
said Owen.

A frog plopped into
the pond and rings
spread out in the water.

Under the water they could see sticklebacks and other small fish.

A cloud of midges buzzed round Owen's head. "They're making my head itch!" he said.

"Put on your hat," said Mum. "That's a point to you. Midges are flying insects!"

"Ooh, look at that beautiful dragonfly!" said Sara. She got out her pencils and sketched the dragonfly before it flew off.

"Watch your feet," said Owen. "Look, there's a slug in the grass. You almost stepped on it!"

29

Dragonfly

When they got home, Sara checked her notebook. "We saw lots of animal groups!" she said. "And I got the most points!"

"I'll look harder next time," said Owen.

"You can try spotting animals in the garden," said Mum. "Or in the park," said Sara. "There are lots of animals there!"

A fly buzzed past Mum's nose. "There are lots of animals in the house too," she laughed.

WRITE YOUR OWN STORY about a nature walk. Draw pictures of the animals you might see. If you're going on a walk, why not keep a nature notebook like Sara's? Make a chart listing animals in groups.

Mammals	Birds	Insects	Fish	Others
Human	Thrush	Midges	Sticklebac	Slug
Rabbit	Owl	Dragonfly	k	Worm
Fox				Frog

QUIZ

What group of animals do you belong to? Can you name three other animals in this group?

Answers on pages 4 and 20-21

What is the group of animals without **backbones** called? Which member of this group has a shell?

Answer on page 8-9

How do **reptiles** warm up and cool down?

Answer on page 16

Which groups do these belong to?

Milk

Tails and fins

Antennae

Feathers

Answers on pages 12, 19, 21, 23

INDEX

amphibians
  5, 14, 15

bat 20
bee 5, 11
beetle 5, 10
birds 4
blackbird 19
butterfly 5, 10

cat 6, 23
cow 23
crocodile 7, 16

deer 25
dog 4
dragonfly 29, 30
duck 5, 19

elephant 5, 22

fish 5, 12, 13
fly 30
fox 26
frog 5, 14, 28

gibbon 21
goldfish 5, 7

human 4, 21

insects
  10, 11, 23
invertebrates
  8, 9

jellyfish 9

kangaroo 21

larvae 11
lion 5
lizard 5, 16

mammals 5
midge 29

newt 5, 15

penguin 18

rabbit 5, 26
reptiles 5, 16, 17

scorpion 8
seagull 5
seal 5, 20
shark 5, 13
skeleton 6, 8
slug 29
snail 8
snake 5, 17, 23
spider 10
squid 9
starfish 9
stickleback 29

tadpole 14
thrush 27
tiger 24
toad 5, 15, 28
tortoise 17
turtle 17

vertebrates 6, 7

whale 21